Reflections

Reflections

THOUGHTS FROM A SOCIAL TRANSPLANT

Choi

authorHOUSE®

AuthorHouse™
1663 Liberty Drive
Bloomington, IN 47403
www.authorhouse.com
Phone: 1 (800) 839-8640

Published by AuthorHouse 07/10/2015

ISBN: 978-1-5049-2226-5 (sc)
ISBN: 978-1-5049-2227-2 (e)

Library of Congress Control Number: 2015910928

Print information available on the last page.

Any people depicted in stock imagery provided by Thinkstock are
models, and such images are being used for illustrative purposes only.
Certain stock imagery © Thinkstock.

This book is printed on acid-free paper.

Because of the dynamic nature of the Internet, any web
addresses or links contained in this book may have changed
since publication and may no longer be valid. The views
expressed in this work are solely those of the author and do
not necessarily reflect the views of the publisher, and the
publisher hereby disclaims any responsibility for them.

Preface

I decided to write this book for two main reasons.

1. For my family (mainly parents)
2. For myself to help deal with all my stored anger of those early years gone by.

This does not cover the years after college. The main focus is in my early years from the adoption to college and the hints to my thinking/philosophy on life. I think the things I have dealt with can also be of help to other but not limited to adapted ones by any means. We all go through times of trouble for whatever the circumstances. We all have to figure out how to deal with life with what we have and who we are. I decided not to go into to much detail of the issues I had to deal with just the high lights, the things I have overcome, and things that will always be ongoing for the rest of my life. I just wanted to get the general idea of what I went through and while the world moved on without really knowing what kids go through who are not the majority in the social group.

A lot of things have gone on even while writing this book. The social issues are all still out their.

For those who read this I hope you will find yourself and find some laughter and maybe some tears. Life is hard enough alone and sometimes in a crowd you can still feel alone. I am still working on being part of the crowd by believing in humanity, not because I want to, because I need to.

I also want to thank those who have given me my life meaning.

The family I never knew in Texas who sent money in my care for food, clothing and medication when I was in Korea.

To the Adopted Family that ultimately became my family.

To my adopted mother who was my cheerleader in my young life. She also gave me a pallet that would be open to all kinds of wonderful foods.

To my adopted father who gave me music in my life even when I did not want to hear his.

To my Adopted brothers and sisters who gave me sports, love of nature, love of knowledge, and the urge to explore new things.

And to ALL those close friends I had as a child and current. They have shown me trust and loyalty without bounds, True friendship.

And lastly, to all those men and women who have served for this great country I call home.

Introduction: The Early days

I awake to the sound of a child's cry and soon realized that it was mine. Tears left a dried path down my cheeks. Apparently I have been crying for some time. Tear ducks had no more to give like the life I would be leaving behind. As I awake from sleep, I look for a familiar face but find only confusion. Minutes have gone by and nothing appears to be normal in my life. Hearing the whine of some strange device unknown to me soon begins to calm me down and find comfort with some men dressed in white with funny caps on there heads. These men became my unexpected guardians for the trip as I was sent on to a strange new world. A world I haven't even dreamt of lying on a hard cold floor gazing to a ceiling like a young artist canvas, blank and filled with open invitation to fill it with your imagination. They were not assigned to me by anyone but myself and by the kindness in their hearts. I guess at that point I knew wherever I was destined to spend my time would be special and much more than where I was. I never knew who they were nor recall their faces, I just new that they were my friends. Friends that would be with me for the rest of my life and never to be seen again except for that one brief moment in time. At that moment in my life when I had no one and no concept of time or anything else that this world had to offer.

Within my own mind I was on some type of bus, a bus that happens to fly…. whatever that meant to me, I have no idea. I had no concept of flight, other countries, or other cultures. The idea of seeing other types of faces was like watching a sci-fi movie. All the new faces, the eyes, color, and hair was alien. It was no longer like seeing your own reflection on the stream, how the ripples would distort your face just slightly to appear like another looking back… the same yet different. All I ever knew at that time was about the size of a peanut and that the shell of that nut would be my home… my hiding place for peace and healing. It also became my place to think. Like the peanut once removed from the shell, it's no longer protected. My shell was opened and left behind while I was moved to another shell with other types of nuts. Being that exposed nut, naked and bear leaves one to find shelter as to not get burned. I did however find other forms of shelter in this strange new world called America, where dreams can be of flesh and blood, sweat and tears are your symbols of progress and success. I never knew fear even in the new surroundings. Even missing a bus home would not stop me from getting home, walking was a method I enjoyed even when it took me through areas known to be dangerous. As I grew I would claim another mode of transport to calm the soul. As my neighbor took me in on a ride across the land I would call home. He was to yet another guardian to me as we took a ride from Iowa to Indiana and back to home again. My good friend was also on that ride and we have put a lot of miles together in the years to come. My neighbor was and still is, thank God, a very good man. He helped me even when my friends and I did wrong against his property, I for one did not help but I was with them after all and that is as good as being the one to have done it. I enjoyed many good parts of my new life in America and would grow as the country grew, my mind would be filled with wonders from its long history, which in its own right was a short span in the rich history of the world. The riches in my young life were not of money but dreams and wonderment.

I did enjoy activities the kids in the neighborhood would play. These activities were known as sports and through out the years I would begin to get better but I only enjoyed one the most, getting on the two wheels and peddling to unknown directions with no idea how far I would go. This was my time alone to think, ponder what I may become some day; this would be my fortress of solitude. I spent many miles on two wheels in my teenage years wondering the great countryside with so much freedom and openness. A country built on future dreams of people unknown to all and strangers to none and brothers to all those to come. One never realizes what a nation of differences can do when they think and bond as one, those who strive to reach a goal to many that is unreachable, to do the things that are unthinkable, and dare to reach for the stars and be among them where gods have only existed and gone.

I never thought of anything before my transplant to America but the kids and the adults that helped to take care of us. It wasn't the adults that made a difference in my life, but the other kids. Kids that were left behind for unknown reason just like me. At that age it made no difference since we had food and clothing and place to sleep. The things we had were simple and very few. Toys were no more than a wooden top and a string to operate the top. String would double as a toy by itself for one to create various patterns by looping through your fingers kind of magic tricks in many ways. We all new nothing of beds, flushing toilets (…what's a phrush), we pooped through a hole in the floor never sitting unless you wanted to fall in (only if your hiding…phew!). Running water, machines that washed cloths, all these things were nothing in our minds. All we new were wooden floors with a blanket and "we" covered the floors at night. Treats were not of candy but of corn on the cob. These became the things we strived for not for the food but for the difference in flavor and texture. Rice only goes so far, yes it keeps hunger away only way that rice can…. Blah! That bland taste, oh if we only knew the wonders of a small grain of sugar could do to that bowl of rice. Oh if we just had one ounce of sugar that would have made our heads spin into the heavens, but we had nothing to sweeten the meal, again that's all we had. Rice, that substance we called food I know now is the lifeblood for those who have nothing in other parts of the world and yes sometimes a good thing isn't enough.

I wonder how many of those kids ever made it out like I have. I hope every one of them are living a better life then they have every dreamt about sleeping on those cold hard floors. After all, kids should be having fun with other kids and not having to take care of them but help raise them to be adults, as they become adults.

A new Life

My life as I knew would soon fade into the darkness as open arms snatch me up with smiles and warm hearts in a sea of people rushing like ants around the queen. The buzzing of people moving about in a frenzy I have never seen and the sounds that I never heard. Voices coming from nowhere, …bright lights all around me, defending me from darkness that creeps around the fringe where the light is fading. Yet all those people moving in directions with such intensity, with such wonderful symphony of movements. I had no idea of what was to come yet alone what was going on with me. What did all this mean? Why am I in a crowd of strangers, who is holding me and why? Again all I hear is strange sounds from the mouths of strangers, yet I feel no fear being in the mist of all these wonderful things and people too. What is to happen with me now that I am in a land of strangers? I know for sure that I am no longer near where I started my life and if I will ever see it again. Yet I know noting of the place I have left behind. Again…. Thoughts are blank; as if I had any to start with on this journey in we call life.

I don't recall much more about what I know as the busiest airport at the time in northern Illinois. I do recall a few moments in my first ride as we left the area of the flying buses. The bright lights along the roadways (as if I had any clue…), these cars were bright in color and fully enclosed. Yes, I have seen four wheeled trucks and cars but most in dull colors and had the taste of rice (yeah we've been there… boring!) and never fully enclosed. I watched as we passed other cars and trucks with kids peering out the windows as I was but maybe for not the same reason as I. Later driving off the busy highways we made a stop for what I had no idea. Again with the bright lights and people on wheels (what the f*&^…..?k (not that I knew cuss words or the English language at this point)) …Wow! What else can these people do? When we left that place I smelled something I never smelled before (later to be explained as a chili dog…excuse me…the dog did it…). At some point we reached the place I would later call home.

I was taken inside to this palace full of things, things I had no ideas or concepts on what they were yet alone what one does with them. Everyone took seat on what later was known as furniture composing of chairs and a couch. I don't believe I sat in any of those but the floor worked just as well for me with the exception that I had some additional padding under my own. I sat as items were taken out of this magical bag that contained food (chili dogs). I don't believe I had any problems putting those dogs down and chasing them with brown fizzing fluid (root beer). Good thing I was not afraid of trying new things but later maybe my new family would think twice about… phew! I was later told (years later) that they should not feed me much American food right away, that rice would be just fine (whatever! …Another chili dog please).

That my stomach would need time to adjust to new foods and spices. Maybe they just did not understand who I am, person who adapts to change, person who moves ahead, a person who thinks for himself, …maybe…whatever the reason, I took to all the new things that this new life had to offer. Soft beds to sleep on (blanket and floor would be enough…rriiight!), a toilet to relieve oneself without the notion you might fall in if you lose your balance, the idea of bathing in hot water that you control with a dial (not a sun dial), I also took in the idea of going to school shortly after arriving. I knew I had to learn the ways of this culture to have a sense of belonging or just to fit in as best as possible. I learned to communicate... that was key to my early months. Although my first sign of communication was a simple gesture, a simple finger pointing towards the item or items was very effective but had its limits. I over came all the things that people from the agency said it would take time for me to adjust and to take it slowly. Ha! Again, what did they know! They say that food is the way to a mans heart, it can also be said that food is the key to a young child's dreams of success, of freedom, of life ever lasting.

My mother for all those years she tried to make my belly happy! She cooked up meals that were tempting for any pallet but not always mine. I would become to appreciate the foods that would be presented at the dinner table even when it did not please the nose but could dance a mean jitterbug once on the welcome mat of sustained life. That dance would take a ride to maintain the furnace of life as the body fades to a state of limbo where dreams are manufactured so that we may pursue them once again in the physical world we live in. Food! What is it that we crave so much and why? What defines it as good or bad? What defines it as food? Its life we are all consuming to survive in this existence in the hope we can move onto another? When we look at life and what it means to live we have no real answers but to live as it comes, to take life from those things we consume as food, are we the last in line for the cycle of life before life itself is recycled? So then we eat to provide for ourselves but also to our future.

So then life is the real key to our survival. We need to maintain the food chain that exists in order to keep the doorsteps to a full belly open and the dance of life flowing in our bodies. Not just the bodies that exist now but for the ones that have yet to come. When I first tasted something more than rice and what it meant to be alive in a world beyond the boundrys I would later become sad for those who live on both sides, on the inside they know of nothing more than a simple way of life but on the out side many are taking things for granted that could easily help someone else survive another day. I know not what I do but I know what I do can make a difference all around me and even beyond my reach. The food I have come to love so much is a killer as much as it saves lives. I never realized how much I cared about having food available to me until the day that my plate of food was dropped onto the floor. For that second it took for it to hit the floor, I felt it was my last that I would ever taste. At that moment I almost started to cry when I realized I could still get more food unlike my past life. That day made me think, even when I don't have much, there are others who still have less to eat and would even enjoy eating the food that just hit the floor. After that moment I made a choice that even when I don't have much I would make an effort to pass on money to help feed those who need it. I have been known to give money to those who ask even for the reasons they give me knowing that it's the wrong reason but they still deserve the chance to live and fill their belly. Yes I have enjoyed having the variety of food presented to me by my mother who did everything she could to keep me from closing my mind on the world I left even if she never intend to. If there was one thing my mother passed onto me is to keep an open mind when it came to eating food. Just like people are different, so are the foods that people are eating. They can all be enjoyed and loved. Don't judge the food by the smell, appearance, but give a good taste before making your decision and don't just try it once, try it again some timer later and then make your final decision. People are in many ways like food, they sometimes smell funny (good or bad), sometimes look funny (good or bad), and sometimes taste funny (usually not intentional to taste someone), and they sometimes sound funny but we all are not alike just like the way the same food is made differently by each and everyone who cooks. We have character and so do foods, and like food I have different tastes and have different kinds of friends. Without the love and appreciation of food I would have a hard time to enjoy the people I have met in my life. One might say that food is not just a way to a man's heart but also a way to look at life and the people around you.

Food wasn't the only thing I learned to appreciate. I learned to approach my curiosity with some caution. There were many new things I have never seen or dreamed of. Power tools to me at the time meant I use the tool and I provide the power. Well, this was a new world after all full of magical visionary oddities I wouldn't even dream of. I walked out to see what my stepfather was doing in the garage (a place where a motor car slept) and noticed this spinning device he just used to run some metal against that produced little flying light particles (sparks). This device was just turned off and knowing I have never seen this type of machinery and knowing noting about the way it works just got the best of me. Since my stepfather was able to produce those fancy dancing lights why couldn't I? And since I didn't know any better I used my thumb... can you say OUCH!?! ...Can you say dumb ass! Hell! What did I know of these things? That day I also got to see the emergency room (one of many visits) of a hospital. I'm not sure if I cried, but of what I know, what I did was not the right thing to do. My thumb still reminds of that day. If I was not crying at the time but by the time they started to stitch my thumb back up I would be in tears, tears flowing like the rain in a monsoon. The pain of getting it cleaned and numbed were the worst of it. Stitches were noting more than an inconvenience. I did have the best thumb to go with my clown costume for my first Halloween. Some clowns have a big nose some have big thumbs. From that I wanted to know how things worked and would take things apart just to see if I can put it back together in working order even if it was originally broke. Just as life is a puzzle we struggle to assemble all the pieces without a picture to go by, only what we see through our eyes and mind (life, some mental and emotional assembly required…). At this point my mind has been opened up to so many possibilities and much more to come in the years ahead.

Birthdays and holidays

There is something about birthdays; particularly mine I hate to celebrate. Even my very first one I just never understood the meaning of celebrating your birth every year. Even as an adult I still don't care for it. I will always make the time to help celebrate everyone else's when possible. I have enjoyed the ones I have celebrated with my family as a child but maybe not in the way that most kids do. I enjoyed it because we were all together, the gifts were of course great but from someone who had nothing as of family and friendship, the gifts are a distant third and the cake was of course the best to a distant second. After all, it was one time a year you could enjoy all your favorite foods (yes, thinking of food yet again! ...LOL! (Laughing-out-loud)). To me every day is a celebration of your life/birth and every day you wake up is a reason to celebrate. Some may never understand that and those who have noting making it to the next day is a curse and a blessing all the same. Why celebrate just one day out of the year when every day is another day you live! Life is a gift from the universe, just like the vast universe we know very little and little of ourselves. Life should be celebrated till we take our last breath.

I grew up celebrating my date of birth year after year in my new home but wonder sometimes about those I left behind. Those kids never get special food on that special day and gifts too. Maybe that's why I don't care to celebrate much and enjoy celebrating others because of those other lives I knew back in Korea. Again, I will never know.

Life is a strange thing to define to most since we never really try to define it. If we were to define the truth about life and what it means we may be disappointed in what we discover. Maybe Monty Python had it best or Shakespeare in his tragedies of forbidden love and such over whelming hatred, or the Greek stories of Gods and men fighting over a mere mortal woman. However it maybe defined in each one of us will be our own, but we celebrate our life every day willingly or not, knowingly or not we do every day. Life is not a gift but a reason to live. Gifts come and go, life never truly ends, only the physical presence and the memories of each other we have left behind.

I never understood Halloween, I mean, what was the point of dressing up?? After the first year I then realized it was time for kids to collect free candy so the parents could tell you not to eat it. Come on, what's the point if you can't eat it? I did go out with friends, run around the neighborhood on Halloween like a bunch of crazed kids desiring candy. I don't recall going out that much after the first couple years. I did however enjoy going out with my friends' kids every Halloween years later. Seeing them dress up in the great costumes their talented mother would create for them every year. I have gone out with them every year since the first and soon the time will come when they to stop the ritual, even they must grow up as we all did (well, most!). The first major events in a child are not just the foundation of that person's character, but the beginning of that defining moment of whom that person will be when they are at the age of reason and Halloween could be darn right spooky!

As I mentioned I was a clown the first year and maybe that was my beginnings of my humorous side of my life. I clowned around a lot as kid in school, a side that my family really didn't see. I can't really tell you what else I was for Halloween beyond the first. I know I wasn't a clown every year and some may say that I am still a clown today and every day. I know now that all hallows eve is not what we think of as a child collecting candy.

So each celebration is not always the same and the meaning also may differ from group to group, country to country, and person to person. One of those is the biggest eating day of the year, the day of all days for those who only ate one thing in life would think they have died and gone onto a better life. For those this would be greater than Christmas. Yes I am talking about Thanksgiving, The day that is known best for stuffing yourself to the point of exploding. Foods I never heard of nor dreamed of. Turkey? What f&%#^ is it? ...Don't care; it tastes great (but not quite less filling) ...LOVE IT! Just pass it on down! Yams and hams yet no green eggs with that ham, jell-o that is so mellow and even some yellow for your best fellow whose about to bellow... please pass the Stuffing! I thought that was what I did with the rice every day, stuffing it down my gullet every day. This new stuffing, well! Pass it on down too! Did the turkey eat this stuff? I can't believe anything that would be this tasty be made by hand of man. Who would think of stuffing a bird and cooking it? All this great food that would be served for kings and queens are laid out in front of me now to consume at will. I guess this world has some good things about it. It wasn't just about food at this house; it was also about friends and family for this particular feast. Yes there was the family but my parents always had good friends and extended family. I really liked the idea of sharing such bounty with which you don't see that often day-to-day life. I would appreciate Thanksgiving even more when a college professor (whom is now a great friend) would invite international students who couldn't afford to fly home to his table to share his feast with his family (...that's a story for another day). I enjoyed those days; it gave me a sense of humanity that is good, a sense of purpose to be alive. Just because you don't have a lot in life doesn't mean you have noting to share or to give to others. This was after all ...THANKSGIVING! Not a time to give thanks but to give thanks to others so that they may live well ...so that we may all live well for what we have or don't have.

Thanksgiving should be a time of reflection of the things you have, the people you have to share with and those who may someday join in the country's national celebration. This after all was a symbol of the first shared meals in the early days of this country and the native people of the land. We owe a lot to those who have shared the bounty of this land. It is good we carry on the tradition of those early days and hope we never forget why those who gathered that day. They were not the same but different and welcomed strangers to their land. This country has and I hope always will be a land of dreams for many new comers to come and give thanks.

Speaking of things to have or not, I found Christmas to be a mixed time for me. I understood the idea and concept but as I grew up I did not understand the point of or the irony of telling kids a story of Santa Claus. Come on, a man in a red suit that travels around the globe delivering toys in twenty-four hours? Maybe I thought too much about it but maybe it was the moral issue that lay under the story. Why tell kids not to tell lies and yet at a very young age we are telling kids one of the biggest lies of all. Intensions are all good but long lasting affects could be bad. Kids will eventually figure out it's people very close to them and through the parents god hears the good and the bad that confirms what God has already seen and heard. We say his son died for us but how can someone truly die if he is remembered and honored, by celebrating his birth; when in fact we are celebrating his death, or are we really celebrating our wants? We all believe in some higher power, but what we call that higher power is not the same name throughout the world. My belief in Christmas has faded in the years as a young adult and has never come back as an adult. I believe in the concept of being good to your fellow man and sharing the peace and harmony that

13

our world offers to each and every one of us. One of the last things I had done with my grandmother and mother was to attend a midnight mass. We found seating and shortly after all the seats were taken a pregnant woman comes up. I look around and see that it's standing room only. No one behind me or in front of me would give up his or her seat. As she looked around and as our eye's met I offered her my seat and asked her to sit. I found it very displeasing to see a church full of religious people not willing to offer her a seat when a woman was so close to having her child. Where was the spirit that night? I would have done this even if it were not Christmas Eve. I was raised to do the right thing even when no one has asked to do so. Where has Christmas gone...? To make things worse even my mother looked at me as if I was nuts to give up my seat and stand for 45 minutes or so.

Don't get me wrong, I loved the presents I woke up too on Christmas day but it faded quickly after a few years. The biggest holiday of the year now all about how well the corporate giants do so they can stuff the pockets of the board and executive team, so much for the spirit of life.

Next big event was Easter. I can understand celebrating rebirth of life after a long cold winter but lets face it dealing with the Easter bunny was not exactly what I had in mind if anything. No wonder why I always heard kids crying when faced with a HUGE bunny. Good thing I was old enough to understand that it was not a real bunny. Seeing a six-foot bunny is a scary thing and yet we were told that the Easter bunny would bring us gifts as well.

Here we are again with more gifts but this time it's to celebrate the rebirth of our planet and all things living. No wonder why kids are asking for things around the holidays.

I too have grown to be of "wanting" of things but at the same time understood that it was not good to be "wanting" things, and yet I still want things. I don't expect things to be given to me, but that I should earn those things that I want. I am just another person in society, a society that is loved by many and hated by others but misunderstood because all they see is the political views of the men and women who lead this society and not the heart and soul of this society. Our leaders do not always speak or represent the whole but the partial, more like the splinter from a large board. That represents a very small fraction of the people. There is something more to holidays than gifts; we all just need to discover what that is in our own way. A six-foot bunny is not an answer to the rebirth of our planet nor a representation, just another way to teach a lesson on life. The bible teaches us that Jesus rose from the dead and ascended to heaven with the sins of man so that we may someday join him. I hope wherever we go, it will be a place of peace. Kids these days are growing up with no beliefs in life and worst of all, themselves. We as adults owe it to our kids so that their kids will have a chance. If all we ever leave behind is a better way of life for our future kids, then we can proudly say we are giving them a chance for a better life than our own.

The fourth of July celebration is one that I just enjoy especially after I became a citizen of this country. I understand that this country had to do things to become what it is today. We became a country, a country for others to believe in, a place to call home, a place to standup, and a place to be heard. Some sacrifices had to be made by many to give to others. This day is a reminder of where this country has come from. Why it does what it does for others. The best part is of course the fireworks. What a way to cap off the birthday celebration of this great land! How many in this country really understand the principle upon the nation was formed? Many are to busy fighting themselves for something they already have…. Freedom! Instead of offending others we need to embrace them as much as we have embraced the holidays in our country.

Learning and Sports

Social events and belief systems were not the only things I learned the first year, I also was introduced to a sport that I would love even to this day and shared with people in my life. The first time was not what everyone would think and those who have done this with me since would not understand. I never made it to the Olympics but never planned on it either in this event. I was introduced to down hill skiing; this would be one of my favorite winter events. Being strapped into a pair of boots and then bound to a pair of long, flat, wooden sticks looked crazy and going down a mountain sounded even insane but fun! ...Yeah, what are you thinking? ...You idiot! My oldest brother took me but the bunny hill just wouldn't do for him, he took me straight to the top! Thinking back now I should have gone with my sisters instead...maybe I might have learned something (like staying alive). So the first lesson, don't go straight down, and what do I do? Go straight down and the marks on the mountain were not the only marks I left ...that you could see any way. Ok maybe just fall and crash in a big ball of snow cloud trailing me as I go down the hill was a better description of my first run. Lesson number two, go side to side to keep your speed down. Fine! Just how do I do that as I plant my face into a tree (not really, just came close). Lesson three, put one and two together as you go down the hill. Piece of cake, HA! One thing I learned as a kid was to learn fast and soon I was on lesson four with my other brother, moguls and jumps! …What the F%^!$@% am I thinking! Good thing it wasn't all on the same day. Oh and as my father and mother ski by, do the "snow-plow" (better known now as the wedge) to slow down and to make the turns easier. So there is a concept to this whole thing and doing all of those things in the precise amounts so you can maintain speed and control to go down the mountain while gravity accelerates you faster and faster… HOW DO YOU STOOOOP!!! Those were great times. I think the first time of doing anything (sports related) is always be the best time you will ever have …in hindsight!

I still love the sport and even tried to teach a few people I have become friends with or met through other friends. I would never forget this family activity for the rest of my life. It has always defined me to never let things get the best of you; you are in control of what happens to you in life. Getting back on the skies after falling is easy, pointing yourself to the bottom of the mountain and pushing off towards your goal is hard to do for the first few times. You just have to get over it! Do the easy thing and let yourself go. This is also true in life, at some point in life you will need to let yourself go from the chains that bind you.

Sometimes in life you just need to let yourself go and enjoy what life has to offer at that moment in time.

The next sport or activity I learned was in water! Ok maybe it wasn't a sport but activity. Learning to swim.

We had a swimming pool (not that I knew what that was) in the back yard. A good size in-ground pool with diving board. I'm told it was good exercise for my brother in "water rescue" at the time. After the pool was opened that first year I was at my new home I saw my brother and his friends having fun in the pool. I apparently had to join in on the fun. I jumped in and sank right to the bottom! Like a rock! Good thing it was in the shallow end but I didn't know any better to stand up. I just knew the water was over my head at this point. My brother jumped in and got me out as I was expelling water since I had no idea I couldn't breath under water, so again with the lessons. I think we all get the first one, don't try to breath under water! Apparently I was not afraid of water either... after all, I rode a bus over a large body of water.

My oldest sister instructed me on the concepts of swimming. I can't say I've mastered any of the various strokes in swimming but enough to keep my head above water long enough to catch the next breath. Many things did come easy for me but growing up with new faces and never seeing anyone like you only in a mirror never bothered me until school. I spent many days in the water since the first day, it was a great way to stay fit and playing tag with friends were always tiring working your entire body in and out of the water.

I did go onto playing other sports such as basketball, football, cross country and track and field. I wouldn't say I was the best at any of them. I will go into each one a just a touch more in the proceeding pages as my learning process develops since I learned these things while learning my three "R's.

Playing catch up was never in my thoughts. I have expected myself to be an equal among the kids I would soon face every day. Never would I allow myself to be left behind whether games, academics, or sports. I would perform all things well until I have a clear understanding of what I will become in life. One would expect a child to be timid when thrown into a lion's den faced with new challenges at every point along the way. Did I speak the language? Did I fit in? Did I look the same as the rest? Did I dress the same? Did I smell the same? Did I... I never considered playing that "did I..." game at any time. Where would that get me if I wasted time on such trivial things? After kindergarten I would face one of my toughest years, first grade was not only challenging but also cruel. Here I am in a classroom full of kids and a nun that would push me to hate the educational process. Maybe it was good, maybe not. I have learned to deal with it but not in a way that adults would have preferred. This was the beginning of holding things in and mentally dealing with it in my head. Where it would sit and smolder until a door or window was opened to feed the hot ashes to a roaring fire. How was a child that could not speak the native language explain what has happened to him? How is that child to understand what he is being punished for since he could not fully understand what he did right or wrong? I went through a lot that year learning to speak the language and trying to keep up with the class in the basics, the fundamentals of the society, and the educational requirements to move on. I know I did well but I also know that I did things that I have no ideas what I did to get in trouble several times. This wasn't just playtime trouble; it was also academic work I did not do correctly (I had very little understanding of what I was doing but did the best I could). This went one for the entire school year and by the end I was starting to understand my mistakes but not the punishment and embarrassment of the punishment carried out in front of the entire class. I don't think my parents knew or understood that first year of school. The year that put me more in a shell than any other event up to this point. I dug in deep and never really came out until much later in life. I now had the true feel of what this new world can bring, cruelty, happiness, and triumph over those who knock you down. This is when I first felt different, which one of these is not like the others…. Yes, that was me **DIFFERENT!** I could no longer think along the lines we were all equals, the same. Even though we are all different within our own social ethnic groups.

It wasn't my fellow classmates that caused me most of the grief; it was the older kids, the kids between my grade and my brother whom I looked up to. Kids in my brothers' class did not treat me like I was different; they accepted me far as I knew. Kids come to me mostly when I was alone or one other kid near me to call me names and disfigure their eyes to look more like mine. Calling me yellow and this was long before mellow yellow came along. As if I even had an idea what "yellow" meant. I barely knew it as a color let alone a metaphor for skin color and whatever else. I could be having a time of my life at school and the next minute I am taunted for no reason that I could see nor understand. I just knew I would close the door and hide and let that small spark dance in the darkness of my mind until enough sparks light up the darkness. This buildup could last weeks, months and even years before the big bang! And boy what a BANG it was each time.

This was not all bad; I would start to value friendship as I started to understand it more and more with each kid I would meet. Kids in my class were kind to me, maybe they were just afraid I knew karate and would use it on them. Hell maybe I did maybe I didn't. I would later use that to my advantage by not answering kids who ask if I knew it or not. I started to make friends that would come and go in my young life, some lasted longer than others and some would just be classmates and nothing more. I never had any problems making friends but I think in some cases I never did make friends, they were just intimidated by me and my size (I was a big kid). Better to be on my good side I guess then not. That first year as they say was an eye opener!

As you might have figured from the Nun, I attend a small Catholic grade school (patron saint of hopeless causes). My second year in many ways would redeem the educational system. I could have never asked for anyone better than Brother Doug. He has shown a lot of compassion and love for teaching kids, not just about religion but also about kindness. Maybe they had a routine setup to get the kids in line the first two years in the school. If they did, it worked well on me. Brother Doug would be one of my favorites in the educational system for the rest of my life. His teaching of right and wrong, forgiveness, selflessness, compassion and love of making kids happy through teaching was seen every day. Don't get me wrong, he did punish me a few times but not in the manor of THE NUN! I made it through the first two years with flying colors even with my troubles with older kids, which I kept to myself. Most of my classmates I don't think had a clue on what was going on between some of the upper classman and myself.

My next year would be yet another year that would bring new feelings into my life but would not understand them until years later. I made progress in defending myself, no I did not pick fights but those sparks glowed warm enough that those particular kids started to notice that they are pushing their luck. I did however push a few kids around to establish my rank in the classroom and beyond. I figured out that I could take advantage of my size to decrease the amount of tension around me. I never picked a fight, just a few looks and motions were enough. The other side to this year in education I was yet lucky enough to have my first teacher that was not a Nun or Brother. Her name was Candy and was special to me in ways I didn't understand. I hung around her as much as I could. I was told that when on a field trip to the zoo I never wanted to let her hand go. Maybe out of some fears of the animals in the zoo or some other reasons yet not discovered in a young boys mind and imagination. I do recall holding her hand a lot that day. All I know for sure I was lucky to be in her group and not with another classmates mother and maybe it was planed that way. I knew she was special to me and meant a lot to me just didn't know why and how. I learned even more about friendships as well. My close friend at the time would eventually move away to a big college town due to his fathers' new job coaching baseball. Through his dad I got to meet one of the great players of the game Ernie Banks, picture and autograph included. By the end of 3rd or 4th grade I would have lost my second best friend that I've had in my life. Yet through the year I would always be close to Candy and always we would share laughter or two each day. I still liked her even when she made fun of me in front of the class. As the year was coming to a close I would find out that she was getting married and her husband to be was a funny man. He and I would also share many laughs in the short time I knew him. I would see him years later come into the store I was working and he still remembered who I am. The last laugh we had that year was during a school event she entered me in the cool-aid drinking contest without me knowing it. Boy did I have to pee after that! She later found me and I asked her if I could go to the rest room, her reply was... "It took you long enough..." I also had to run a relay race after the contest. One of the playful things I did to her was the Doritos crunch. I shared a chip with her and as she bit down on the chip in front of me I fell backwards to the floor. The look on her face was timeless. She knew I got her!

The last day of school was somewhat of a mystery to me at the time. As we were all heading to the doors of the school to go home I was talking to one of the girls in the class that I liked (I mean I liked!) I noticed she was saying good-bye to all the kids and the girls were giving her kisses and she was saying good-bye to the boys until she got to me (I was the last one out). She had put her arm in front of me to stop me and turned me to face her and asked if I had anything for her (kiss?) and I just turned my head and she kissed me on the cheek and said good-bye. These days an innocent kiss would be mistaken for something greater than it is. This wasn't the end of her teaching, she would be back for many more years there before I would lose track of her. I wish I knew what I know now then… When I stepped out the door my brother and neighbor have seen what just happened and you know big brother just wouldn't let that one go.

I went into 4th grade and played basketball and made a new best friend whom I would later teach how to shoot a jump shot. I was the center on the basketball team and he was the point guard. We had a great friendship while it lasted until public school in 7th grade. I also lost my first hero to drugs, my brother. No he really didn't die, just in my mind he did. I looked up to him more than he ever knew. With those things going on in my life, I was still making friends and getting less harassment from others but not gone completely. It really never goes away, just the people do. They mature or they too learn what its like to be on the receiving end. I never had problems making friends even when I new the person is at the receiving end of a missed milk carton as it soars until it hits the cheek of the new girl who just transferred in. What a welcoming she got that day. She and I did get to be good friends through high school. As 5th grade came in I also made new friends around the neighborhood and would be one of the key influence for me to go to a public school. Not just for the education but for the sports. I did do well in sports and the private school only had basketball. I would also start finding interest in girls around this time and there were plenty to choose from. Never understood what attracted, what girls saw in me. I never had problems talking to girls, maybe because the older girls would come up to me in my younger years to squeeze my chubby cheeks and say how cute I was ...oh I miss those days! A lot has changed since then a lot has changed now. My parents can attest to my evenings talking on the phone several girls every night for hours all through junior high. This wasn't the end of seeing my favorite teacher in the hall, just a longer span of time in between. As I said I did switch to a public school. The two girls that I talked to the most also switched as well and my best friend at the time too. This also meant I would lose touch with blonde headed girl that I liked so much but she never knew I did. It was change for all of us, larger student body, more new faces, and for me another year of teasing during lunch hours when I'm alone with no friends to sit with for the first month. Sports were my savor this time. I made more friends out side of the few I already knew from the neighborhood, the kids who convinced me to participate in the other sports that were offered in my new school. I would do well but academics were at times a challenge. I still have not mastered the English language, speaking wasn't a problem; writing was problem and still is. I knew by this time that I could do whatever I wanted to do and how well I wanted to do. This was the start of me controlling the grades I would get. I would usually do enough to get by and apply myself only if I needed to except English and grammar; I had to struggle just to get a passing grade.

This was also the year that my hero started to fall away from me. I looked up to him for all those first years of my life in America. Yes my brother went to the dark side of life. I don't know if he ever new the role he played in my young life and how his actions have affected mine. Sometimes things help you in life choices and the directions you will head without you really knowing it. My brothers actions opened my eyes to the signs of drug use and care free life style. Did it make me a better person? Did it make me weak? Strong? …or just informed? Whatever the case maybe I am who I am from those detours in my young life, life goes on with or without you, hero or no hero…It is amazing how ones life can be changed by a single person and that person can never know the role he just played in another's life. We can all make a difference in someone's life every day even if we have no intention to do so.

I started to play pop Warner football in sixth grade on the urging from one of my neighbors father. He enjoyed watching the kids in the neighborhood play and wanted to see how well I could do on a team. I wasn't sure about the whole thing but after his sons got into the act I talked to my parents and so did the father of my friends. I thought it would take much more convincing than it did. Football with pads was much different than playing during recess or in the back yard with friends. Contact was much harder and being dragged down to the ground and times thrown down was nothing to be desired but was part of the game. I did all right, was I a starter, no and did not expect to with all the talent there was on the team. They already had a great running back that knew the game well. I was just a backup tailback and free safety. I did do well my second and third year of playing the game. I came to rely on my teammates too do their part in the game as they relied on me to do mine…. scoring (attempting to any way) touchdowns. I was only good as what people said about me, you would have to ask them if I was any good.

By this time I also started to ride bicycles for distance. This was my summer thing to ride and reflect on my life and to ease any mental pains I have. I also joined the cross-country team, which was uneventful. I had more success at track and field. I was primarily sprinter and also a long jumper. I had a few wins in a sport I never thought I would participate in. Junior high was a good time for me in sports and meeting new people, people who not only enjoyed the after school activities but the people who were on the team. I had a lot of good friends just from sports alone. I would also have a good time with the competition before we go head to head in our events, true sportsmanship. Its funny how young sportsman can ALL are equal and friendly but once outside of the field of competition all that changes. Why? It doesn't have to change we are all still equals!

I may have been a popular kid but I still would get teased by some that seem to think its funny to pick on kids, to push their luck on the chance nothing will be done back to them and always when they have friends with them, never alone. It seems when you put your guard down you eventually find yourself in a scenario from the past and it hits you hard and even harder as the years go by. Just being in the "in crowd" doesn't exclude you from the teasing of racism and ignorance. Most people I knew would never mess with me just because they know I can be mean and cruel and not worried about being bigger or smaller than anyone. Some knew or had an idea what I could possibly do. I never let my emotions get the best of me, and most people knew when to stay out of my way no matter the age.

The first 8 years of school have taught me a lot about character, integrity and who I am. Sports have taught me about teamwork and representing a group not just on the playing field/court but also off in public. I did do well enough in track, basketball, and football. I did well for the ones who enjoyed watching me play the game. With the team sports I learned what it meant to help and encourage teammates to excel. To help those who come out to support you because through you they live the sport.

Junior High came and gone with the passing of time and memories tucked away for another time for another generation to come. High school was just around the corner and yes more sports. Summer was filled with rides and swimming with a side of tennis and one trip to Indiana for a track and field meet with a group of upper classmen. We camped out that night and woke early the next day. Unfortunately for another and myself we had

2 hours of sleep. We ate a great breakfast to get our day going before relaxing before the start of the meet. Warm-ups, stretching, light running to get the blood flowing from head to toe. Heart pumping to keep the parts fueled with oxygen. Luck would have it we all did very well and I pulled off late charge to win by a hair (photo finish). Some had counted me out as I came out of the turn but I managed to finish on top. Back home with our spoils of war and egos fattened up for the up coming year.

School started with the usual greeting to your friends that you haven't seen all summer and most of your close friends you've seen at practice. The girls a bit more filled out and some just exploding out. Then there are the old faces you've seen from junior high who are now sophomores and yet more new faces all round. Then BAM! My first class and here we go again with the trash talking form the upper classmen. Right off the bat he has to dig into my appearance. I ignore him for the time being and catch up with others in the class. This wasn't a special class, just shop. For me I wanted to know more than just the three R's. I eventually get back to Richie later in the year. I had enough with him since my seventh grade lunch hour and now as a freshman during lunch he still talking smack! Well I've had enough; he starts in with his friends behind him calling me names and such. Lets get it on! You have nothing to lose and I have everything to lose. So lets go right now, right here! I may not win but I know I will get a shot or two in for sure. Yes I had friends around me too but they were not going to do anything except urge Richie on to put out or shut-up! Over at the table of teachers they know something is going on but they do not move form the table, just watching to see what happens next. Luck would have it BIG Richie was all talk and no fight. Good for me but bad for him, he had to back down in front of his buddies. I know that my friends would have helped me if I asked or if they felt the need to back me up. Others I knew just wanted to see what I was made of. Well, no one really found out anymore than what they already seen, nothing! Nothing has changed, I was still the unknown as a tough guy and I would always remain that way. All they knew I was strong, quick and things did not bother me for the most part. That's all they needed to know. I would however learn to watch out for those who would not watch out for themselves or couldn't. I was a student leader (PE assistant) for PE classes. We would help with examples and help to keep the kids focused. However, once in awhile you will see fights or even worse someone picking on anther person. I've had to intervene a few times with one particular kid who just picked on the weaker kids and there is always one. I've had to restrain him and let him know that was not going to be tolerated by me and any other leaders for this class. I did what I did maybe because I know what its like and I knew I had to watch for others as others have done for me.

After that event my high school years were uneventful. I would quit a few sports my junior and senior years due to coaching ideology that did not coincide with mine. Only sport I was in for the entire four years was track and field. I was not the most popular kid but known none the less. I really never cared what people thought of me and never wanted to know. I had several girl friends except my senior year but had many very close female friends and would be considered best friends and one I loved like a sister. The one I was very close to was one of the most desired by many in my class. The girl was near perfect, as any young man would want. We enjoyed the time we had, the time spent together and apart. As I reflect, it was perfection. Together in those years that I knew her, people ask if we were a couple. The answer was always no, just very good friends! She was one that every guy wanted to be with and I had the honor to be her good friend that spent a lot of time with. We laughed always, embraced in a hug when one had a bad day. I would find a way to make her smile on those cloudy days. I had many good friends both male and female alike.

Even when I was no longer playing in the big sports I still felt I was a part of the team. I even quit the game that I loved the most, basketball! I still love the game but don't like the way it has changed since I played. I still play with friends when we can. For me to quit the games was a tough decision to make. It was a part of my American heritage; it was America in many ways for me at that time. It was what I had to do, I had to adapt to each opponent, learn to play as member of the team, learn to play my role, learn the roles of my teammates, to lead when needed, and follow the lead of others. Learning to do those things not only made me a better player, better teammate, better student, and most of all the best person I could ever be. This ideal of being the perfect young athletic student built to fight, to win by playing your best to be the best.

Playing my best was always my goal in all sports but not academics, academics were second to pleasing others. In other words, it wasn't in my top ten. Win or lose I had to be at my best. I did my best I win even when I lose, not my best, I lose even when we win. Their has been many times where I felt I never played my best and I win or the team wins and I would be upset about my performance, like I let the team down.

If there was one thing I did not do was to celebrate a win, a score, a touchdown even if it was a game winner. I let that be done by the team for the team. I've never been a person to show much emotion even to this day. Not that I don't have any, I just enjoy the smiles and laughter of others.

Others have always come before me even before coming to the states. I have never been much of a solo act but enjoyed being in the solitude of self when I have it. I don't consider myself a loner but I do enjoy spending time for myself and those friends I have close to me understand that. Understanding me may not be the simplest thing or the easiest. Understanding me is the key to knowing me. Understanding others may be a key to understanding yourself. As a kid I didn't need a parent but I needed a friend. I grew up taking care of myself for the most part and friendship has always kept me sane. Friendship is above all living life with others like the notes on a sheet of music, sometimes you get it right and sometimes you don't. Nonetheless it is still music.

Who am I?

There are times when one looks in a mirror and sees the reflected image of him or her self. Now what goes through ones mind may not be what they think is reflected back from the looking glass. I have many times at a very young age looked and was proud of what I saw. It wasn't perfect but I knew that I have come such a long way from where I've started. Knowing another language, knowing nothing of the world I matured in, and who I would become entering adulthood. No one ever knows what is to come in the years ahead. What they have seen and done in the past maybe a clue to where they are headed if they are paying any attention to where they have been. Unfortunately most are to busy paying little attention and only focused on having fun. There is absolutely nothing wrong with having fun and living a carefree childhood but you eventually will need to stand on your own two feet.

I never had an issue to stand on my own and that I think made me more independent and thinking I can survive on my own with very little help from adults. Its not that I did not get along with adults, I got along great with them, well maybe except my parents as most teens do. I'm not sure what the adults seen in me but I for most part had their trust (at least that's what I thought). I knew what I wanted to study in college, had my vision of how the profession I choose should be. Maybe I was setting myself up for a let down…I have a dream of success, reaching it and understanding it is another matter.

As I starred at the image in the mirror I would see a child, others who saw me growing up would see a young man. What was the difference that I did not see? What was it that distinguished myself to get that image from adults? Clueless! Yep, that was me, CLUELESS! Even though I had many of my own thoughts on how things should be, how things should work. Things sometimes just surprised me because they worked or functioned in a manner not in line with my thoughts. Don't get me wrong, I wasn't some great thinker but someone who always had some wild ideas going though his head ever hour of the day. The only thing I didn't think much about is my schoolwork, as I mentioned I only did enough to get by most of the time. This never made my parents happy so every now and then I would put just a little effort into academics. Playing dumb is much harder than you think. I controlled what I do and how I do it. I know I can do whatever I wanted and as well as I wanted. When it came to thinking I was always had an idea. Most people never knew nor really wanted to know. I would get involved with some who did ask about my thoughts and truly wanted my point of view. Surprise was usually what they got; it wasn't always the way they thought I would respond. This kid was full of surprises.

My body did mature quicker or earlier than most kids. My voice was deeper, I was taller and out growing my shoes and clothing until about seventh grade then I stopped. I was at my height by fifth grade. I was stronger than most since I was always doing something for my dad that required physical activity more than just mowing the lawn. I was always in the swimming pool, ridding a bicycle or even at a young age walking to where I needed to go. I never let anything stop me from what I wanted to do. I was a problem solver even at a young age. Maybe the problems were anything major but at that age everything is.

I've had heartbreaks and also the greatest feeling of all of being wanted. Most may not have an idea about what goes through a child's mind when they realize they are not naturally part of the family they are with and eventually become of age, not the age of innocence but the age of knowing. Knowing not right or wrong, knowing they were left behind by the ones who gave them life. For that unknown is the darkness in a child's mind and heart; the lack of care, being held by biological mom or dad, and the comfort that comes from the ones who will protect you from the outside world at whatever the cost. The one great thing, the unconditional love is gone. They are left alone to fend for themselves no matter what the age of the child. It's much easier when that child is a new born and planted into a family and easier to explain when the parents passed on for one reason or another. The one thing that drags us down is why? For me that wasn't much of a question. I didn't care because all I know I had to care for those kids that were younger and smaller than I. The ones who have been transplanted outside of diapers have a much harder time since we are already aware of life. Again the most important thing for anyone in this situation is friendship. We all understand friendships come and go but true friendships are always with you beyond the genetic boundaries' that everyone sets. It truly is a greater bond than blood for those who have no natural family. I had one such friend that I could rely on every day and never complained. This friend was a cat, a cat that choose me by running up my leg every time I walked into my friends garage. When my parents allowed me to have it, it followed me much like a dog. She would only listen to me and sit on my lap. She was always there on my bad days lying on my chest. She was loyal to the end.

I never really thought much about why or whom my natural parents were, where they may be if still alive. I had to respect my adopted parents for what they did even when I had no idea what was going on. I tried to be the best child anyone could ever have, to be the perfect child that could be (if there is such a thing). Did I ever reach that goal; I don't think so. Did I make them proud? I hope so. I never wanted to bring up the subject about my natural birth parents and never enjoyed talking about it in front of them or anyone else. I have my life and I cannot start playing what-if game. Then you have to ask, what if he was never adopted? I may have become more successful. One never knows what the future holds. It was better for me to leave it alone and live my life the best way I knew how. Move forward and never forget your heritage and be proud of being part of your new country. Be proud to defend what it stands for and what it gives to those who have come for a better life. I have also come to appreciate the men and woman of our arm forces. I know if it wasn't for them my life could be much different. I do what I can by always donating to the cause to support the veterans and current members when I can. Remember those people who gave us the freedoms we enjoy and willing to die so that we may keep living the freedom. Those men and woman are also part of my heritage. They have fought on the soil that gave me life, to ensure the freedoms of others in need of protection.

I think people forget about where they came from, whom they represent. I'm not talking about those who were born outside the states but the ones who look back into history and use that as their means to get ahead. You can't forget your heritage or your ethnic back ground. I don't claim to be an Asian American but an American and proud to be. I will never forget where I came from or where I was born or the people that I once belonged with. I cannot live in the past if I want to succeed in this life. In order to succeed you need to push forward here and now and to what could be tomorrow. Living in the past will only bring bad feelings of hatred, heartbreak, misery, and regret. Moving beyond the past you still need to keep in your mind as not to forget because that is where you will get your passion to move on and to succeed. No matter who you are, take a good look in the mirror and ask yourself "who am I?" you may be surprised on your response or lack of response. It may take us a lifetime to figure out who we are as individuals and as a group, as a society.

As I realize the successes in my life and the failures, my thoughts still wonder into the darkness, to my imagination still trying to find myself. I am much like Clark Kent as we all are, just without the super powers. We both grew up as strangers even when accepted by the locals but still different. We both came from a world apart, did not understand who we were and why? We had to put up with a lot from others and yet still found some success with the locals. We both had to endure the pains the new world laid upon us and fight to keep ourselves together. The pains that others will not understand except those few who have and still are searching for that one thing…acceptance. Yes even superman had his issues but eventually started to be accepted, and I too with others like me (in my situation) would eventually be accepted by most. I have been fortunate enough to be gifted by the close friends and family I have now and for those that have touched my life. Like Superman, we would both be molded by our past and polished by our future to come as a new citizen of these great UNITED STATES. Much like superman we both believe in our adopted country, not because we are like the others, because we are different. It's the difference that makes this country great and why our founding father's named our country the way they did "These United States"!

Many may think I owe something back to the ones who took me in. I would be one of those if I had a voice in that decision to take a stranger into their home. Well the thing is, I was never part of that in any way. I know what you're thinking you were just a kid! Kids, even kids can be bigger than life when the need arises. I never knew what was happening to me; for all I knew I was going to be in Korea for a long time. I did not know what was to be ahead for me. If I knew I'm not sure if I would have gone, after all who would take care of the kids? I've always been a giver rather than a taker. My father and I had a disagreement after my sophomore year of college and as I was leaving he said, "You know I didn't have to adopt you?" and my reply was, "Why did you?" Still to this day I have not heard the response. This does not excuse what you may think of me but after all these years one might expect an answer during the time the lines of communication were open. People say things in a heated argument but that could also be the truth coming out as well. I always hear what people are saying, I had to!

I've always been a good listener for my friends, for my classmates and teammates. To understand others you need to first understand yourself (I know I've already said these things). If you understand yourself others are easier to understand but then again some you just can't. I don't always agree with the way people think but I have to respect their thoughts because we are all human and as humans we will always make mistakes. Some of us learn from those mistakes and other never do and some it just take a few more errors. No one is perfect as along as we are human and we will never have respect for each other until we move from our past and look to our future as one race and stand together to help one another with no regrets, no questions, and nothing in return. We all need each other to make it past another day and wake to another tomorrow. When we wake we may understand the reflection just a little bit more.

...Thoughts from a social transplant.

Choi